MEMORIAL

OF THE

New York Mail Steamship Company,

OF THE

CITY OF NEW YORK,

TO THE

Senate and House of Representatives

OF THE UNITED STATES

ON

OCEAN STEAM NAVIGATION.

MARCH 1864.

NEW YORK:
LATIMER BROS. & SEYMOUR, LAW STATIONERS 21 NASSAU ST.

1864.

MEMORIAL

OF THE

New York Mail Steamship Company,

OF THE

CITY OF NEW YORK,

TO THE

Senate and House of Representatives

OF THE UNITED STATES,

ON

OCEAN STEAM NAVIGATION.

MARCH 1864.

NEW YORK:
LATIMER BROS. & SEYMOUR, LAW STATIONERS 21 NASSAU ST.

1864.

TO THE HONORABLE THE SENATE AND HOUSE OF REPRESENTATIVES OF THE UNITED STATES, IN CONGRESS ASSEMBLED:

THE MEMORIAL OF THE NEW YORK MAIL STEAMSHIP COMPANY,

Respectfully Shows:

That your memorialists are prepared to enter into a contract with the Government of the United States to carry the mails by regular lines of steamers, between the port of New York and the ports of Havana, New Orleans, Galveston, Point Isabel, Tampico, Vera Cruz, Saint Thomas, Martinique, Para, Pernambuco, Bahia, Rio de Janeiro, Montevideo and Buenos Ayres; and they solicit the passage of an Act of Congress to authorize the making of a contract for that purpose.

Your memoralists respectfully represent that they are an incorporated company, organized under the laws of the State of New York for the business of Ocean Steam Navigation, and have power to prosecute their business on all the routes between the several ports above mentioned; that they have a capital and surplus of seven hundred and fifty thousand dollars, and they have the means of increasing their capital to any amount which may be required for their operation; that they now own and have in use two steamships, and they have in process of construction two other steamships; and that they intend to maintain the following regular lines, namely:

A main line from New York to New Orleans, *via* Havana, consisting of five first-class side-wheel steamships, of from 2,000 to 2,700 tons burden, and sailing from each port once a week, and making fifty-two round voyages in each year.

A branch line from New Orleans to Vera Cruz, *via* Galveston, Point Isabel at Brazos Santiago and Tampico, consisting of two first-class side-wheel or screw steamships, of from 1,200 to 1,500 tons burden, sailing from each port every alternate week, and making twenty-six round voyages in each year. This line is to connect regularly with the weekly line of steamships between New York and New Orleans.

A main line from New York to Rio de Janeiro, in Brazil, *via* Saint Thomas, and Martinique in the West Indies and Para, Pernambuco and Bahia in Brazil, consisting of three first-class screw steamships, of from 2,250 to 2,500 tons burdens, sailing from each terminus on the first of each month, and making twelve round voyages in each year. This line is to be increased to six steamships, and is to make twenty-four round voyages in each year; and also, to include a branch line from Rio de Janeiro to Montevideo and Buenos Ayres, whenever it shall be required.

The distances to be run upon the several routes are as follows:

Main line—New York and New Orleans, *via* Havana........................	2,135 statute miles.
Branch line—New Orleans and Vera Cruz, *via* Galveston, Point Isabel at Brazos, Santiago and Tampico...............	1,240 " "

Main line—New York and Rio de Janeiro, *via* Saint Thomas, Martinique, Para, Peruambuco and Bahia..............	6,370 statute miles.
Branch line—Rio de Joneiro to Buenos Ayres, *via* Montevido...............	1,370 " "

Your memorialists offer to contract for carrying the mails regularly upon all those routes, for a period of ten years, for the following prices, payable periodically as the service shall he performed, namely:

For the main line between New York and New Orleans, *via* Havana, total service to be performed in each year, 220,040 statute miles, and the branch line between New Orleans and Vera Cruz, *via* Galveston, Point Isabel, and Tampico, total service, 64,480 statute miles, together making 286,520 statute miles, the compensation to be $175,000 per annum, or at the rate of sixty-one cents and one mill for each mile of service.

For the main line between New York and Rio de Janeiro, *via* St. Thomas, Martinique, Para, Pernambuco, and Bahia, total service in each year 152,880 statute miles, the compensation to be $150,000 per annum, payable by the United States, upon condition that the Government of Brazil shall pay for the same service the further sum of $100,000 per annum: the total compensation amounting to two hundred and fifty thousand dollars per annum, or to one dollar sixty-three cents and five mills for each mile of service; and when semi-monthly service is required, the compensation to be increased to three hundred and fifty thousand dollars per annum—which would reduce the compensation to one dollar fourteen cents and five mills for each mile of service.

For the service upon the branch line, from Rio de Janeiro to Buenos Ayres, *via* Montevideo, when required, the compensation to be at the same rate per mile as shall be paid for service upon the main line between New York and Rio de Janeiro.

From the interest which has been manifested by the Brazilian Government in the establishment of a line of steamships between their ports and New York, it is not doubted but that the sum asked from Brazil will be readily granted. During the past year, a proposition to grant a subsidy of one hundred and ten thousand dollars to a North American Company that would perform twelve round voyages during a year, between Rio de Janeiro and New York, calling at the ports of Bahia, Pernambuco, and Para, came within six votes of becoming a law. The recent elections in Brazil have brought the liberal party into power; and there is no doubt that when the proposition is again considered, it will at once be approved. The people of the United States have a far greater interest in the establishment of this line of steamships than have the people of Brazil; for by it our commerce and our exchanges will be directly benefitted—new markets will be opened for our manufactures, and a great nation closely united with us by the bonds of commerce.

The steamers calling at St. Thomas and Martinique will there connect with the several lines of the Royal Mail Steam Packet Company and of the Imperial (French) line to all points in the West Indies and the north coast of South America. At Para, it will connect with the lines of steamers running upon the Amazon, upon which the transportation of passengers and freight for Peru is rapidly increasing. There are now well-established English and French lines of steamships, between the ports of Brazil and Southampton and Bordeaux—both under subsidy from their governments. In 1850, Great Britain established the first steamship line to Brazil, and from that time her commerce (which during ten years previous had not increased) has increased very rapidly, until now the English merchants maintain almost a monopoly of the Brazilian market for manufactured articles. The American Consul at Rio de Janeiro, in a recent letter, enclosing a report of the commercial condition of Brazil, and referring to the diversion of trade from the United States, says: "So long as there is no direct steam communication between the United States and Brazil, just so long will our nation occupy the present humiliating position in regard to the control of its commerce," and adds, "that the trade with England and France has grown enormously, and almost beyond belief, since the governments of those countries established regular monthly steam communication with Brazil."

The regular mail-steamer, so essential to the vast business correspondence belonging to foreign commerce, has become a necessity of the age.

At the same time, the compensation given by commercial nations to their own steamers for carrying the mails, is indispensably necessary to the shipowners as a part of the means of supporting and maintaining their operations. The profits derived from the transportation of freight and passengers are not sufficient to sustain first-class lines of ocean steamers, except upon short and well-established routes, upon which business is large and constant. The aid of the Government, through its payments for carrying the mails, therefore, is the necessary means of securing two great objects of public interest, namely, prompt and regular mail communication, and rapid and safe transportation of property and persons.

Your Honorable bodies wisely have acted upon these views, in some instances, and immense advantages have resulted from such true and enlightened policy. The present state of American commerce is such as to invoke a liberal exercise of that policy and to call for efficient governmental aid. Other nations have gone far in advance of the United States in encouraging and thereby establishing lines of ocean steamers. British,

French, and Spahish steamships, with the aid of government subsidies, have established their lines upon the North and South Atlantic, touching the American coast and islands at points from the mouth of the St. Lawrence along the shores of North, and Central, and South America, to the mouth of the La Plata; and trade which the United States, as the nearer neighbor, and in closer political affinity with the countries of this continent, should have secured to its citizens, is thus diverted to the merchants of Europe. The same means which have drawn to the old world so much trade fairly belonging to the new, when rightly applied here, will return that trade to our merchants and build up our own commerce.

Your memorialists respectfully call the attention of your Honorable Bodies to the extracts from a letter (which are appended hereto) writen by the Hon. A. C. Tavares Bastos, a leading member of the Liberal party in Brazil, and addressed to George N. Davis, Esq., an American merchant at Rio de Janeiro, in regard to steam navigation between the United States and the ports of Brazil. The letter from which those extracts are taken was recently published in a New York Journal.

As an example of the energy and liberality of other governments in sustaining their lines of Ocean Steamers, your memorialists ask your attention to some of the subsidies paid by the British Government for the carrying of mails in ocean steamers. That government pays as follows:

To the Cunard Line........................$2.38½ per mile.
" The Royal Mail Line.................... 2.46 "
" The Peninsular and Oriental Line......... 1.53½ "
" The Australian Line..................... 2.75 "

Our own government has paid as follows:

To the Collins Line........................$3.10½ per mile.
" The Aspinwall Line..................... 1.88½ "
" The Pacific Mail Line.................. 1.70 "

It will be noticed that the prices proposed by your memorialists are at lower rates, being 61$\frac{1}{16}$c. on the principal routes, and \$1.63½ on the others.

The great actual prosperity of our country, notwithstanding the burdens of the present war, and the hopeful and assured spirit of our merchants and navigators, render this a favorable time for largely increasing the business of ocean steam navigation. Your memorialists, in the early stages of the war, before our fleet had gone up to New Orleans, not doubting the result of the contest, began their work; they have made a fair commencement; and their steamships, the *Morning Star* and the *Evening Star*, running between New York and New Orleans, *via* Havana, already have acquired a reputation to which your memorialists beg leave to refer as some evidence of their capacity and fitness to carry on this great enterprise.

In assuming the enlargement of their plans, so as to include all the lines upon which they now offer to carry the mails, your memorialists hope that your Honorable Bodies will extend the customary favor of a mail contract, to encourage their undertaking.

And your memorialists will ever pray, &c.

Office of the
New York Mail Steamship Company,
161 Broadway,
New York, March, 1864.

Robt. J. Hubbard,
Secretary.

John Raynor,
President.

Extracts from a letter written by Hon. A. C. Tavares Bastos, Brazil, to George N. Davis, Esq., Rio de Janeiro, on Steam Navigation between Brazil and the United States.

MY DEAR MR. DAVIS:

Your letter has given me great pleasure. In addition to the honor of your attentions, I must express the lively satisfaction which I experience at the interest which you take in our (the Brazilian) great question, viz., direct steam navigation between the United States and Brazil. I must also express my thanks to his Excellency the American Minister, for giving me a portion of his time in regard to this most important measure.

* * * * * * *

"What would be the largest sum which I judge the Brazilian Government would grant as a subsidy to a direct steamship line with the United States?" I reply that it would be the duty of our government to give the sum necessary for the undertaking, whatever that sum might be, from the fact that it is a matter of vital importance to our agricultural interests that we enter into closer relations with the United States. I proposed last year the sum of $110,000 as our share of the annual subsidy.

* * * * * * *

The ease with which our government could aid by a satisfactory subsidy to the company that will unite Rio de Janeiro, Pernambuco and Para with the markets of the United States is acknowledged by all. Unfortunately, to speak frankly, there are some pretended statesmen among us who wish to disseminate in high and official quarters a sentiment adverse to relations with the United States. These adulators, in order to show themselves more monarchical than the monarch himself, insinuated that Americans will revolutionize Brazil; that if we form intimate relations with them that they will finish by annexing the valley of the Amazon. Happily, however, the opinions of these suspicious spirits of darkness, who alone have made our darkness more dense, have been falsified by the good sense of the people of both countries. For we meet with Americans in all parts of Brazil, and principally in the valley of the Amazon at Para, where they nourish commerce. In Rio de Janeiro

Americans have rendered commerce the labor saving machines of their agriculture, which is analogous to ours. In the province of Rio de Janeiro our great man of enterprise, Sr. C. Ottoni, confides to Americans his vast undertakings. Sustained by their indomitable perseverance and extraordinary energy they have in the second division of the Pedro II. Railway filled up valleys, perforated through the Serra de Mar with tunnels, and at this moment locomotives made in their Northern home take possession of the heights over Thermopyla.

Excuse the emphasis with which I express myself. This is a subject which incessantly occupies my soul. I wish to influence the destinies of my country by pointing out the era of transformation, moral and economical, in which my native land needs to begin by establishing direct steam navigation between the two countries.

Brazil needs *new blood*, she needs the *Yankee* spirit, this intrepidity, this energy, this masculine spirit of invention and progress. She needs to re-model her Portuguese and priestly prejudices in the world of generous ideas of liberty, as to-day we cast rifled cannon from the old fashioned and worthless culverins. * * * * * *

But I forgot that the most effective arguments are commercial interests. I have already, in a work published last year, referred to this subject. Commerce between the two countries is constantly increasing. In 1859, we imported from the United States, to the amount $6,000,000, and we exported to the United States $22,000,000. Now who is the most directly interested in the closer relations of which I have spoken? Without doubt Brazil, and above all the planters and dealers in coffee, and the collectors and merchants of the India rubber of the Amazon Valley. If the sum total of transactions in the normal annual period, and without the aid of steam is $28,000,000, is not the advantage of a steamship line between New York and Rio evident to all?

No one can foresee the increase of importation from the United States when there shall be the great convenience of steam communication with New York. To-day no one ignores that Americans begin to take the lead in our markets in certain articles, which they compete with and surpass the English. The

United States furnish us with breadstuffs. You have even imported for us Indian corn in years of scarcity. Many articles of furniture and of wooden ware we buy by preference of the Americans. Yes, even in the mountains, whence I write this letter, I have seen many household comforts which we call American. The Pedro II. Railway Company have formed so good an opinion of your foundaries and machine shops, that they now prefer American locomotives (Baldwin of Philadelphia) and American cars (Wasson, Springfield, Massachusetts.) The English, who almost monopolize our market in cotton and woolen fabrics, send to Brazil articles of a high price and inferior quality, hitherto without competition. Would that American manufaturers would obtain information of this great market, and by studying near at hand the wants and tastes of 9,000,000 of people I have no doubt that in a short time they would be strong competitors of the English. Who would profit by this competition? Undoubtedly the Brazilians and you North Americans.

Another consideration. Brazil need civil engineers, men of enterprise, intelligent laborers, men habituated to new inventions, and they themselves inventors. These precious men abound in the United States. Brazil offers herself to emigrants.

Let American steamers navigate the Amazon; let the coast trade be free to the starry flag and to friendly nations; give impulse to railways and the navigation of all our large rivers; above all, let us have a line of steamers between the United States and Brazil; and then we shall see the development of our country by an advantageous influx of Americans.

If we insist upon this question it will soon triumph. The occasion is opportune. The recent arbitrary conduct of England excites in the whole of Brazil a great disconfidence in all European governments, and by this means some of the most obstinate minds have been opened to the idea of an intimate alliance with the United States. The moment is propitious.

And now, my dear Mr. Davis, feeling that I have not been as useful in this matter as I desired, with profound respect and the greatest esteem,

I remain your servant,

A. C. TAVARES BASTOS.

Province of Rio de Janeiro, March, 1863.

MORNING STAR.

www.ingramcontent.com/pod-product-compliance
Lightning Source LLC
LaVergne TN
LVHW020641110826
845149LV00004B/1304

* 9 7 8 1 4 1 8 1 9 0 2 8 6 *